TRA

Tips, tricks and ideas for the female traveller

STACEY ANDREWS

Do it. Go.

Some people bungee jump, others get their thrills from shooting up drugs. We take a plane to another city, another country, where we don't know anyone, or where we might stay, what we might see - we don't even know more than two words of the language! We become addicted to the sound of suitcase wheels on the airport floor and the clicking of backpack straps buckling up for wild adventures.

We open our eyes, open our hearts and open our minds. We let places engulf our five senses, while they steal little pieces of our soul. We learn more than being in a classroom could ever teach us, and realise, we will never look at home, or the world the same way again.

SMILE!

"A warm smile is the universal language of kindness."
– *William Arthur Ward*

Well, yes, usually. But in some countries, mainly Eastern Europe (Russia, Poland etc), your friendly smile as you leisurely pass someone on the footpath can be mistaken as superficial, or you just escaped from the looney bin.

You can test your own waters if you're trying to smile sweetly at an officer when you 'really did not know' your bus ticket had expired before you travelled.

"All that is gold does not glitter,
not all those who wander are lost."
– J.R.R Tolkien

"But I need my dose of Vitamin D!"
In the summer months only a few minutes of sunshine in the morning and afternoon is usually efficient to provide your body with Vitamin D. Sunscreen also does not affect the amount of Vitamin D your body receives. Australia and NZ are at the top of the ranks for deaths by suncancer, due to sitting under the Ozone hole. Other places like Colorado have high UV levels because of its altitude, or countries closer to the equator e.g. The Phillipines also attract stronger, more dangerous levels of UV.
To prevent being a leathery old bag, or walking sun cancer, apply sunscreen 15mins before exposure- especially swimming. It's also good to remember that UV levels can be higher on cloudy days, or on reflective surfaces like the snow or ocean.

Windburn can also be painful especially in places like Patagonia. Use sunscreen or moisturiser and a scarf to shield yourself.

'If you can't afford insurance, you can't afford to travel.'

Never sick? Never lose anything?
At least take the basics so the small cut that turned into an infection or the drunken guy that stage dived off a ledge at Tomorrowland and crushed your foot, doesn't require your parents to remortgage their house.

"I've found out there ain't no surer way to find out whether you like people or hate them, than to travel with them." – *Mark Twain*

A Scarf.
Keeps you warm.
Prevents sunburn.
Eye mask.
Head dress.
Sling.
A towel.
A bag.
Pollution mask.

"I feel like walking the world, like walking the world." – *KT Tunstall*

Bus Rides

In (very) foreign countries:

- √ Try and get a seat on the window above your bag to keep an eye on it.
- √ Never leave anything in the part above your head. Thieves use extendable hooks at the back of the bus to gradually pull your things along closer to them.
- √ Expect to pay a little more for having luggage underneath.
- √ Don't expect the bus driver to tell you it is your stop.
- √ Try and have the correct bus fare to avoid ticking the bus driver off or not receiving the right change.
- √ Often the satellite on your Google maps will still work without internet so you can try and track where you are.

Ryan Air and other airlines charge up to $100 if you do not print your itinerary.
Check all of your fine print, twice.

TRY IT

Go surf, snowboard, learn a language, write a book. If you never try, you'll never know. No one cares (or remembers) if you succeeded, except you. And more often than not, you will surprise yourself.

"Did you ever notice the first piece of luggage on the tarmac never belongs to anyone?"
– *Erma Bombeck*

Be alone for a little while. Find happiness and solace in yourself.

Drugs

Coke, cocaine, biff, white horse, powder, crack, wacky dust, big C, crystal, paradise white - no matter where and what it is called you are going to travel to countries where drugs, in particular cocaine, is going to be a lot cheaper and more available.

Yes, they can enhance a party night, or ruin one. Use your head- don't take drugs off strangers, and if you are, remember they can be very different from home, easy does it! People do build up a tolerance to drugs, in particularly cocaine, so while old mate that hasn't left the hostel for six months is racking up three lines a time, half of that is enough to put a non-user out for the night. Don't forget you are in a foreign country, police can be stricter, and hospitals harder to find.

DYK - A standard Australian drink has 10g of ethanol, whereas a Japanese standard drink has just fewer than 20g. Muslim countries such as Bahrain and Saudi Arabia prohibit alcohol. Other Muslim countries including Morocco and parts of the UAE can make it hard to obtain, or very expensive.

Vegetarian Vs. The World

The word 'vegetarian,' can be very unknown in many countries such as Bosnia, Argentina and Greece.

"No meat, no animal," at a restaurant can often be returned with a look of bewilderment, soon turning into pity.

These countries can even be a meat overload for your everyday carnivore, having the foreign traveller searching high and low for a decent salad after a few days.

Many countries will have bread as an entrée and if you're a vegetarian you soon learn this will be your main intake. Always check prices of sides and entrées before tucking in as they sometimes inflate these prices, even though they look free!

Mmm bread all the time, you will feel as bloated as the Michelin Man in no time.

Top vegetarian-friendly countries to visit are Turkey, UK and Thailand.

Government Gaga
eft wing, right wing, chicken wings??

ıe words socialist, republican and ıııore come up often in the news and traveller's conversation. This should get you through.

Democracy: The rule of the people. People vote for those who govern them. Countries today- Australia and Canada.

Monarchy: The King or Queen have absolute power. Was more popular back in the day. Countries today- Brunei and UAE.

Republic: Very similar to a democracy, but there is a President instead of a Prime Minister and the majority doesn't always rule. Countries today- USA and Austria.

Communism: An economic and political system where the government owns most businesses and resources. The wealth is divided equally amongst citizens or where required. Countries today- North Korea and China.

Dictatorship: Where absolute power and control is held by one person. Famous deadly dictators include Saddam Hussein and Adolf Hitler. Some say the leaders of Russia and North Korea are running a dictatorship.

Anarchy: No government, absolute freedom for the individual, often resulting in chaos, rebellion and misorder. No current countries with anarchy, although there are some areas in Mexico and Greece.

Left wing/socialist: People who believe in welfare systems, protecting minority rights and usually have the future in mind.

Right wing/conservative: People who value tradition and believe that they should keep their money to themselves. A survival of the fittest point of view, where business shouldn't be heavily regulated.

BE CULTURED

Travel.
The University of the World.

Who are the United Nations?

The United Nations were developed after World War Two to promote international co-operation and preserve peace. The UN started with 51 countries and now has a total of 193 countries.

What do they do?
The United Nations do not make laws. It is there to resolve international conflicts and create policies on matters affecting all of us.

The matters vary from disease, refugees, telecommunications, protecting the environment and many more.

UN - Interesting Facts

- √ Kosovo, Taiwan and The Vatican City are the only three countries not part of the UN.
- √ UNICEF is an agency of the UN just for children and young people.
- √ UN Peacekeepers help over 150million people across the world.

World Heritage Listed

Another section of the UN, World Heritage, designates places around the world with outstanding universal value to be protected for future generations to value and enjoy.

Venice, Siena and Trentino Dolomites are all Italian world heritage listed sites voted in the Top 10 best by Lonely Planet.

Stonehenge has been voted many times over as the most overrated world heritage listed tourist trap as it small and you can't get close.

Tips to save money:

- Empty your water bottle before entering airport security, and then fill it up on the other side. If you can't find a water fountain a cafe/ shop will happily do it for you.

- Food is not banned through airport security, pack a sandwich.

- Clothes swap with other travellers you meet to freshen up your look.

- It is often cheaper to fly than drive, compare your options, especially through countries like France where there are many road tolls.

- Take a certain amount of cash out with you when you are having a big night out and leave the rest at home. Now you can't spend it all on shouting the bar and 3 kebab family meals on the way home.

"You're going where???" Bellows an angry Grandma down the phone.

"Bosnia, Nan," I reply.

"But there is a war there, they're all killing each other!!"

Yes, about 20 years ago there was. Things have changed, and are constantly changing. Do your own research, get out there, talk to people who have been.
Turns out Nan's dream destination to holiday is Athens- think it may have gone downhill more recently than Bosnia for young girls travelling solo.

What's actually happening in Bosnia... ...Beautiful waterfalls, river parties and bridge jumping!

Guerilla

You will hear 'Guerilla Warfare' or 'Guerilla Territory' in discussions about countries such as the Colombian border or certain spots in Mexico.

It is a good idea to avoid these areas as ambushes, raids and kidnaps can be common by the rebel groups.

Crossing The Darien Gap (land border between Colombia and Panama) is a goal many 'extreme' backpackers aim to do in their life. The 144km trek on foot is known for dense jungle, home to the Guerilla Warfare groups, corrupt police, indigenous tribes and drug smugglers. Many backpackers choose to sail through the San Blas Islands instead.

Latin Lovers

Everyone has their preference; we've all had that fantasy. Spain and Brazil recently claimed the steamy title for the best in bed, and maybe it's the Spanish background, but you can't go past a sensual, strong, dark featured man who can also salsa. Do yourself a favour ladies, but be careful they may also take your heart.
And just in case you need to know, Germans were ranked in the last place.

The journey is just as important as the destination.

Drunk and Disorderly

So many muggings or thefts can be prevented. While working behind bars in Central America and London, a conversation would go like this:

Two French Girls (crying): They took everything-iPhone, money, passport, while we were walking home after the club shut.

Bartender: Just you two girls alone? Why didn't you take the free shuttle back to town, they advertise not to walk because of muggings?

2FG: We forgot once we were drunk.

Bartender: Oh I see... let's not even start on why you would have your passports, phones and everything else out on a 'let's get wasted night.' (This last part wasn't actually said, just an 'oh that sucks').

Customer 1000th in the bar: I hate this place man, full of thieves! They stole my iPhone last night.

Bartender: Oh no! Where was it?

C 1000th: In my back pocket.

Write the name of your hostel address on the inside of your arm before going out for the night if it is tricky to remember.

"Follow your instincts. That's where true wisdom manifests itself." – *Oprah*

Baby Wipes

Perfect for festivals and camping when a shower isn't possible!

"A stranger is just a friend you haven't met ye
– *William Yeats*

Banking

all your bank, you can reverse the call charges.

dit card expiry date before you leave.

Separate your bank cards so if a wallet or bag goes missing you have back-up.

Loose plans are the best plans!
Be impulsive! Jump off that train a few stops early if it looks interesting!

A little more than a standard **1st Aid Kit.**

- Immodium- stops the runs!
- Hydralite- when you are feeling really dehydrated.
- Amoxicillin- if you are prone to bladder infections.

Religious Symbols

The crescent moon and star found on the top of mosques represent an international symbol of Islam.

The Star of David- Jewism/Judaism.

Alpha and Omega - Christianity. Meaning the beginning and the end, God is eternal.

"We travel not to escape life,
but for life not to escape us". – *Anon*

Sandwich bag your phone before heading to a sweaty/rainy festival, or to the beach to stop sand scratching.

Events off the Beaten Path

Glastonbury, La Tomatina, Burning Man, Full Moon Parties and more are hands down amazing experiences, but there are many, many more cool events around the world a little less known.

Envision Festival (Feb/March) - Costa Rica

Festival of Lanterns (November) – Thailand

Carnival Cologne (February) – Germany

Prague Music Festival (May) – Czech Republic

Edinburgh Festival (August) - Scotland

Laundry On The Go

Of course you can wear your clothes more than once without a wash (or even 5 times), but when the need arises, plug a small sink (use a sock if you don't have a plug) and add laundry powder, soap or shampoo. Hand wash your clothes around just like a washing machine would. Let that dirty water out and do it again with fresh water and no soap.

Central American countries can be surprisingly expensive for laundry as water and power prices are high. Thailand and other Asian countries are cheaper per kilogram to have your clothes washed by a local.

Document Safe

ocuments, including passport and them to yourself. Open the email you also have an offline copy.

CityMapper will be your bible in London and other major cities. Download the app to navigate the tube and red buses like a local.

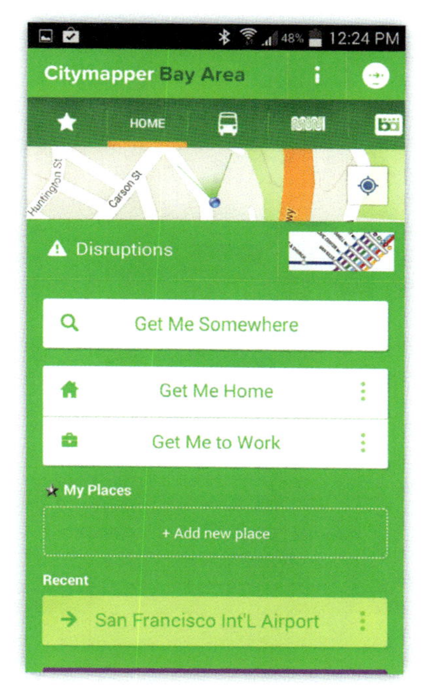

Uber

If you're still paying for taxis in big cities, you are paying too much. Plus, Uber cars are usually fancier.

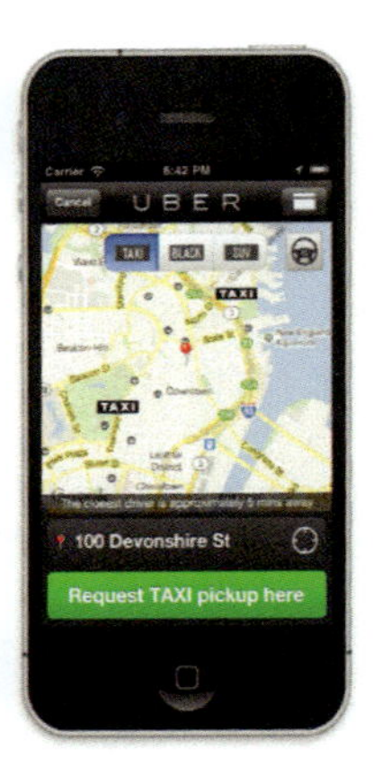

Moisturise!
Changing altitudes and countries seems to leave skin extra scaly and dry.

Loop de loop!

If you are out for dinner or falling asleep on the bus, make sure you hook the handles of your bag around your arm or leg to prevent bag snatching.

If you only book one thing, make it a safe transfer from the airport and your first night in a reputable hostel, especially when arriving at night.

Malaria

is found in many countries, but Nigeria, Sierra Leone and Mozambique suffer the highest rates of death by the mosquito spread disease.

People will often scare you into taking Malaria medication (which can have serious side effects) when visiting countries like South Africa where it is not necessary in most parts. Double check with your travel doctor in your home country who isn't trying to make a penny or two out of you.

Say, what?!

Many antibiotics, including the medication to prevent Malaraia, stop the contraceptive pill from working.

Malaria symptoms

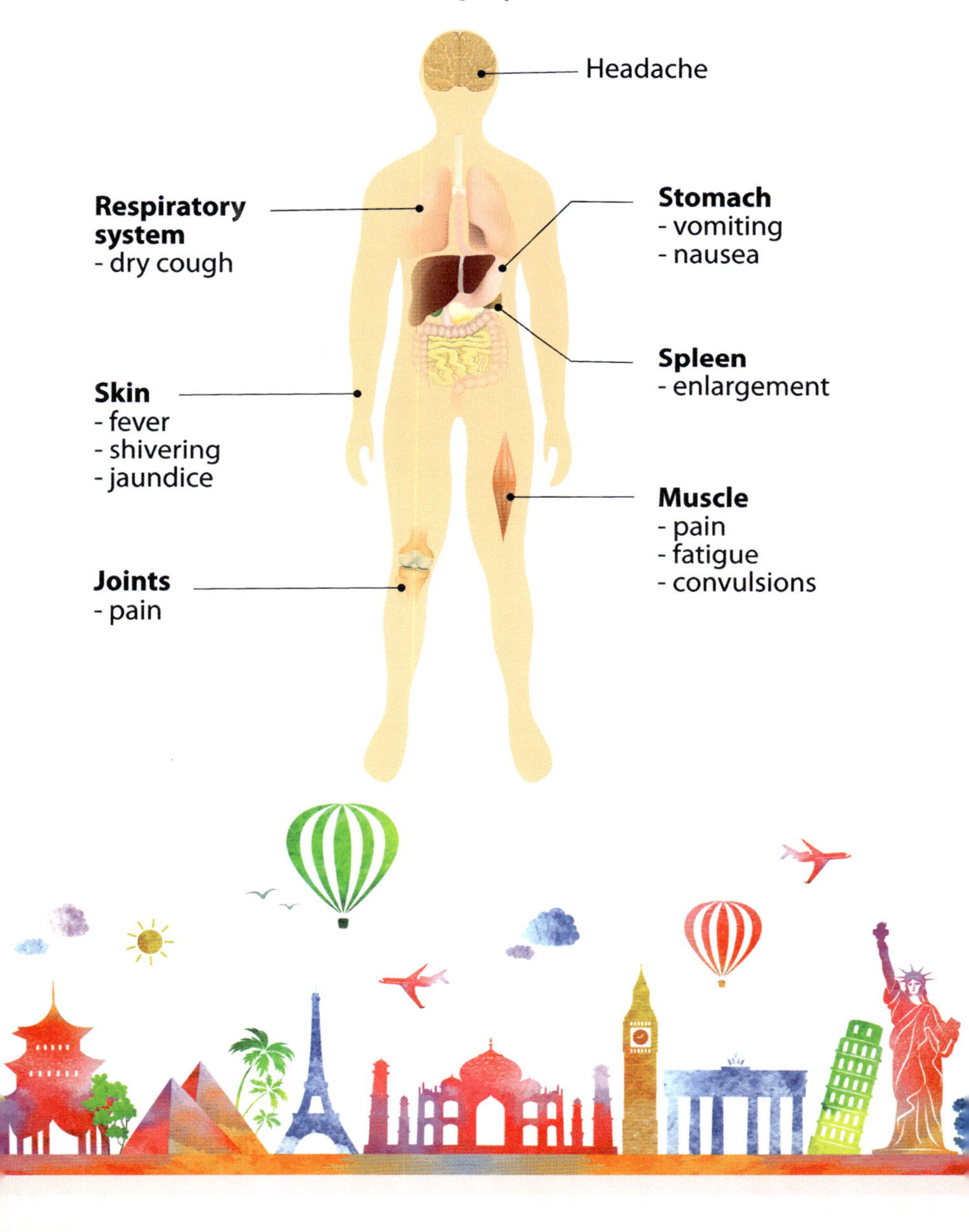

Dengue Fever

Another disease spread by mosquitoes, common in SE Asia, The Caribbean and the South Pacific. Strangely enough, it seems just like having the flu, and passes after a week or two, but can be very serious if it returns in the same person.

Advice? Cover up at dawn and dusk, and love thy mosquito repellent.

"Travel, the only thing you can buy that makes you richer." – *Anon*

Use Dettol Soap as your everyday soap in the shower to prevent any minor scratches becoming infected.

Yellow Fever

You will need to receive your YF vaccine before travelling to countries in South America and Africa. Pick up a certificate to recognise you have been vaccinated or you may be put in quarantine when crossing back into some countries.

Working on the Go

Workaway and WOLFing are two great websites that will match you up with places to work and volunteer while abroad. Jobs can range from vine picking in the valley of France for a season for your accommodation, or teaching yoga on the Caribbean beaches for a week.

Patience is a virtue.

Everything happens for a reason.

It's not about the destination but the journey.

Remember this when you miss the bus to the next town. Or the ATM is out of money. There are so many wonderful tales of travellers having these issues than finding the best town ever because they had to go to the next place to use the ATM etc... And if it doesn't turn out to be a blessing in disguise, having a meltdown wouldn't have helped you anyway.

CASH MONEY

Always keep at least 48hours worth of cash safe with you (two nights' accommodation, a few meals and a bus fare). Usually in American dollars as the green back is accepted and valued through many countries.

One of my favourite hidey holes is to replace a lipstick with the cash.

I recently read somewhere to not get down by looking at other people's Facebook because it is not their real lives, and no one lives that happily.

ARE YOU KIDDING ME??

I'm controlling myself not to swamp the news feed with more sunsets of our bonfire on the Pacific Coast of Costa Rica, or the home-made dinner 'Big Mama,' cooked us up in Mexico. You only get to see a small part of our happy travelling life. It is no cover. I fall asleep and wake up with my friends, or on my own whenever and wherever I want. Okay, sometimes we may have a worry, like our iPod will go flat before the bus ride reaches the beach.

Ohhh hey!!
Yes, you! Great to see you! Yes, I'm waving to that invisible person across the street.

And do it every time you think you are being followed by a stranger, so they assume you are not alone.

"Is that dog really just lying on top of where our food was just cooked?"

"Did that taste cooked to you?"

If you are having a slight regret of eating something off, try drinking Coca Cola straight after to kill the bad germs and bacteria.

Souvenirs

Put it in context of the person receiving it back home. Will it look cheap and tacky? Will they use it?

Try sending the old fashion postcard instead or finding something they will use.

Don't forget when you are packing to leave extra space for items you will collect along the way.

Don't be afraid.

Despite what the media is paid to tell you, it is a wonderful world out there with many more people wanting to meet, laugh, smile and share their lives with you, than harm you.
Use your common sense and you can go anywhere.

In the end, we only regret
the chances we didn't take.

Panty Liners
Use panty liners to double the life of your underwear and keep them fresh on long hauls.

Plastic Bags.
It's always handy to carry a few spare plastic bags for wet/dirty clothes or shoes. Put your liquids in one of these even if they are sealed, to prevent explosions all over your clothes.

Learn to read a map and get your bearings.

1.Ask the receptionist to circle where you are on the map.
2. Stand out the front of the place and take note of other shop names and streets around you. Try and match some on the map.
3. Walk in one direction until you cross a street. Find that street on your map.
4. Try and walk around the whole block following it on your map.

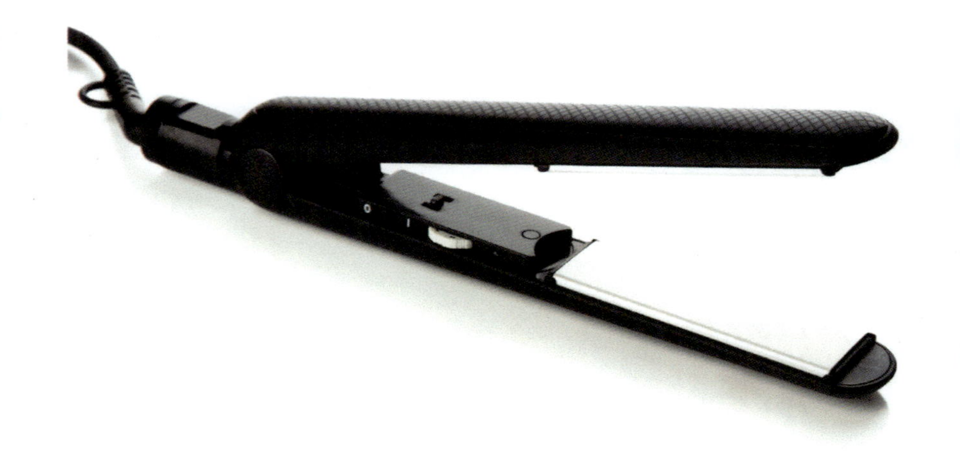

Use your hair straightener as an iron to touch up any crushed clothes.

Always carry a pen with you. Always.

Volunteering

Don't be fooled by big organisations that charge a lot of money for you to volunteer in a country with them- a lot of the underprivileged do not see half of the money you have paid. You can always turn up on your own and head to a local school/hospital and offer your time, or volunteer with a reputable company such as Red Cross.

"I haven't been everywhere, but it's on my list."
– *Susan Sontag*

ams

hat you are statistically safer travelling n you are in your home town, but there scams in every region you visit. Chat with other backpackers and tour guides where you are and they will soon give you the low down.

Nothing is for free. In Paris, they will try and tie a love bracelet on your wrist, or tell you, you are beautiful with a rose, and then chase you down the street until you pay for it. In New York, they will do this with CD's. In Hollywood, taking a photo with the dressed up characters will have them chasing your loose coins.

Negotiate with the Cab driver how much the fare will be before you get in, and ask which way he is going to take you. It is common in Bangkok to go around the block three different ways before arriving at your destination to rack the metre up.
Always take note of the Taxi ID when getting in.

"Oh, that is closed," or, "You missed that bus and there is no more today." This is also a common lie

from taxi drivers to get themselves or their friend's hotel business from you.
Be suspicious of people with large maps asking for directions when they don't look like a tourist. The map can often cover your bag or phone on the table, while sticky fingers you can't see move in on your stuff.

Never give your credit card out over the phone, unless you have called them and know you can trust it. If the receptionist has rung you saying something has gone wrong, go and see them in person.

Don't trust the people 'learning English,' in Shanghai. They want your money, not your friendship.
Fake police- fining you for something that doesn't seem illegal- for example not recognising an international licence when riding a moped in Thailand. Demand for them to meet you at the local police station where you will pay the fine. They usually excuse you very quickly.

If it's too good to be true, it usually is.

Altitude Sickness

The higher up a mountain you go, the less oxygen your body will intake and this can result in altitude sickness. Anything over 2000m can trigger headaches and heights over 3000m can cause nausea and vomiting.

Altitude sickness can lead to fatality no matter how fit you are- always do your research, hire a guide and ascend slowly.

Exchanging Money

You can change money at a bank, outlets or online before you go. You can also use an ATM to take local currency out or you can carry cash and exchange it when you are in the country.

Exchanging in a foreign country:
Check there are no hidden fees.
Use your calculator and multiply the rate and know exactly how much you should be receiving back.
Count the money in front of them before you walk away.

If you are exchanging at the border, be ready with your cash in hand and the minimum amount you want in exchange before they buzz around you like flies. Don't be afraid to say no, and state how much you want.

Once you have your money, jot down how much $1, $10 and $100 is equal to. This will help you when shopping and dining to convert approximately quickly.

Tampons

[illegible]t countries stock pads, tampons can [illegible] to find in some countries such as El [illegible]lvador and smaller towns in Italy and Spain. In countries such as Costa Rica and Pakistan, they are available at more expensive pharmacies and department stores.

Try keeping a stash in your hiking boots or shoes for back-up and they won't take up much room.

Wet and Dry Seasons

If you are travelling near the equator, always check before you travel if you are heading into a wet or dry season.

The dry season is usually the best to travel to avoid flooding streets, closed roads/tracks or the ocean being polluted from all the waste washing out from the mountains into the rivers.

The bonus of travel in the wet season is it is cheaper and quieter. If you take this option, plan activities in the morning as the clouds usually gather with the humidity ready for a late afternoon storm.

A Good Book

Make sure you always have a good book at the top of your backpack. It won't judge you on the days you just want to spend in a hammock from sun up 'til sun down, and will keep you entertained on a 10hour bus trip.

Most hostels also offer a book exchange when you're ready for a swap.

"You will never be completely at home again, because part of your heart will always be elsewhere. That is the price you pay for the richness of loving and knowing people in more than one place." – *Miriam Adeney*

Backpackers and Travellers

You are the best people in the world.
You are interested in cultures of the world and learn to talk and help people, even when they can do nothing in return for you.
You appreciate the smallest, simplest things in life, and never let a beautiful sunrise or blanket of stars go to waste.
You prove that big paid media companies, the government and company executives have got it all wrong. You take the most beautiful parts of the world, appreciate it and bring it home.
You are the people taking steps in making World Peace a little closer to a reality.

Printed in Great Britain
by Amazon.co.uk, Ltd.,
Marston Gate.